Leaf Collection

CLEMSON

LITERATURE SERIES

CONVERSE

As a partnership between Clemson University Press and the Converse University Low Residency MFA program, this series publishes poetry collections, short-story collections, and creative nonfiction.

Leaf Collection

Hannah Marshall

ISBN 978-1-63804-228-0

Cover design by Cath Bruhnke
Typeset in Minion Pro by Gloria Aragon

For information about Clemson University Press,
please visit our website at www.clemson.edu/press.

Acknowledgments

The Banshee: "American Chestnut" and "Home"

The Bombay Literary Magazine: "Cottonwood Music," "Division, Spring," and "Treasure"

BoomerLitMag: "False Cedar"

Booth: "In the Beginning, Forest"

Delta Poetry Review: "How To Be Saved, If You Are a Body" and "Incorruptible"

Four Way Review: "Fable in which you are a barn animal and I am a carnivore"

Hallowzine: "Fulton Street Cemetery" and "Plots"

Hong Kong Review: "Headline, 4-6-22"

New Ohio Review, Best American Poetry 2021: "This Is a Love Poem to Trees"

Pangyrus LitMag: "Atlas of Being"

Reed Magazine: "Diminishing Returns"

Sugar House Review: "Call It Peace"

I am grateful for the support and inspiration I have received from the faculty and staff of the Converse University Low Residency MFA program, especially my mentors Denise Duhamel and Suzanne Cleary. Thanks and love to my mother, Laurel Eshelman, for instilling in me an adoration for the written word. Thanks to the family and friends who have listened to me talk about this book and about all the trees I admire. All my love to Zach and Ramona. I am grateful for every day of our beautiful lives together.

Contents

This Is a Love Poem to Trees

To the sour cherry tree behind our apartment, that summer I made pie and jam.

To the water oak on the coast when you were home waiting, and I said, *Just one more day.*

To the silver maple that waved bare branches twisting gray, when I cried in my childhood bedroom. You and the tree, holding me.

To the linden the summer I was pregnant, and wouldn't that have been a great name for a boy?

Remember that time a raccoon climbed the white pine and built a nest in our dormer, how we wished we could befriend her? The trap in the morning, the drive to the lake, her furry waddle into the woods.

To the woods.

To the tulip tree that wept in early summer, in the new town. The long afternoons I spent alone, drinking tea.

To branches of the old apple tree, alight in your parents' fireplace.

To the weeping willow in Minnesota spring, when I would go for walks and come home, and find you there.

To the mangled green ash outside the window where I sat with our hungry infant. You changed her diapers, and we forgot to touch each other.

To the southern magnolia scenting our neighborhood in Illinois, its fallen leaves brittle as eggshell.

To the bare hickories on our anniversary, ice cream in January, cool sheets and us, alone.

To the hackberry, Siberian elm, river birch, redbud, cottonwood, and aspen. I've loved them all.

To every year the trees grew without us noticing.

Afterwinter

He and I leave the pub
with umbrellas over our heads,
hoping to hear rain softening the cold.
Flakes fill the cups of tulips,
the wet sidewalks,
rain boots.

I wish I'd brought a sweater.
The pond grass droops like a wet dog,
the whole world cracks into a whine, so alive,
crocuses zipped tight, and snowdrops
drooping heavy manes
of ice.

He says of May, *I don't want*
to wish my life away, and here is this snow,
the windows fogged,
the lilacs swollen
with purple milk.

In the Beginning, Forest

A forest was painted onto the cinderblock wall
of my Sunday School room
where the office-bright lighting didn't extend. The sun
sat in the corner, metallic. And the forest
was with God. And the forest was God. The forest was real
when I reached my hand toward it. It was a pine forest,
a winter scene, very Narnian, and I could smell it,
could feel the cold on my fingers. The forest was with God
in the beginning, and I walked there,
where the seemingness of the world
and all the stories and symbols became forest, red needles
crackling on frozen moss. The sun could be stared into
because it was pure gold, and the sky was white as institution,
and the trees were uniform and spoke of pain
when the wind blew. In the beginning, the forest
was Sunday School, and my Sunday shoes were silty
and sturdy, and the forest held us children, and the songs
were the wind and the sparrows. In the beginning, love
was a forest, and the forest was a wild beast. In the beginning,
God was wild and unbound from onion-skin sheaves
and not shut in pine boxes and not taught with fire and blood.
In the beginning, the forest was thick with silence
and could not be named, but even then, I loved the words.

Headline, 4-6-22

For the first time, researchers find microplastics deep in
the lungs of living people—and that reminds me of the
first fleece jacket I owned, teal with snap buttons. There was
time enough, walking the yellow halls of school, where student
researchers watched mold grow in petri dishes, to
find bits of soda cap and nylon fibers on my tongue, a
microplastics constellation, a generation of packaged foods.
Deep stairwell corners where I shared lip gloss in kisses, notes written
in the margins of Vonnegut and Dickinson:
the young think what lasts is them, but it's the plastic in our
lungs which will lie sprinkled about the bones
of all of us, this unwilled detritus, this
living petroleum. Our blood is Day-Glo bright. The
people we love speak sonnets out of littered throats.

Leaf Collection | 6

Observer's Meridian

In the math of astronomy,
a ten-thousandth of a decimal differentiates me
and the robin outside this window,
fluffing her feathers in the crabapple
as March snow washes white the melting world.
She eats the hard fruit, more patient
in her quick little body than I am. And yet,
on nights when the moon is nearly full,
or when the north star rises amid red refractions,
the nadir of my wet vessel seems the crux
of every heavenly orb. Each planet
meets in me, smaller than a speck of dust,
a drowning song of fire—
I can almost imagine my place in this wild.
In the end, such calculations
have more to do with me
than with the myriad burnings of the expanse.
Zenith, what could touch me, what bears
the arc of my receding world?
Fishes and ancient spears, rusting chain-link fence,
a city of barges, blood in snow.
Once, horizon clouded
with the fat bodies of passenger pigeons.
The moon was theirs, and Mars was theirs,
and the Big Dipper was filled with wings.
Now, amid brick and limestone theorem,
the robin ignites toward snow,
and I am alone.

Home

Strange how these things happen—how I can go for the same walk, just up the road to my daughter's bus stop, and then, out of nowhere, my knee won't stop aching for the next three years. Or, seven months pregnant, I lay down on the beach to take the pressure off my hips but stand up stiff and stay that way for ten years. A cyst burgeons on the ring finger of my right hand, insists my attention during seven years of applause. That night when I was nineteen, climbing piles of snow in the parking lot at 3 a.m., I pressed my fists into the softness below my ribs to draw the pain out to the surface. I climbed to the sixth floor and gazed at the concrete, said, *I think you would have me. I'd be petal. Let my weight fall, let there be wings.* My bones scaffolded fear. The swan of my lungs opened and I flew from velvet fingers. True, my heels haven't stopped smarting in five years. My shoulder is a serrated edge in the morning. But I pull the blankets close, home in my body of breaking bits.

A Letter To My Mother

How many times
have you said to me,
about so many different things, *I hope*
I didn't pass that on to you,
disbelief in an afterlife,
a predilection for addiction,
even pubescent lust—but aren't these
just the ways we are human
together? You tell me of the dark bird
perched on your shoulder,
whispering into your ear. And I
have plucked from my flesh
many of your thorns. How you
loved me in all the places
you never learned to love yourself,
but what I wanted most
was for you to revel in your own
body. When you were a child, you washed
your hands until they were raw. You know
the faces fear can take late at night,
and I could see fear reborn on your face
the day of my emergency cesarean,
my legs unresponsive below the sheet.
I lay there, still as swamp water, and for the first time
you missed my teenage angst, all that force
of anger which I would break in white foam
against Dad, even as the water of you
bent around his sharp-edged boulders.
How much of yourself
have you kept for yourself?
This is how I have come to understand myself:
the way my sweaters fit, the way my stanzas
frame the narrative of my life. I was born
into your discontent that hot summer
in Ohio. But I grew up
beside your better dreams, the pottery
studio in Illinois, your infrequent poems
which rooted me in their red mercy
when the lump in my toddler neck
turned out to be cancer. Did you love
or hate my body then? The thing
tearing me apart
was a part of me. Every night
I rest my hands on my stomach,
grateful for breath, and think of you.

For so many years after I left your little farmhouse,
my body seemed not enough.
Winter mornings could tack me down,
so cold I could see my breath
as I rose from my bed. Alone,
I was more like you than ever.
I had to pull the tethers from my veins
just to stay alive. And today, in the gray mist
of your 68th birthday, I look
at my soft face in the bathroom mirror
and try to see you in me,
your comfortable body which was home
to me, your hands with the nails
bitten down. When I confess
a new fear to you, Mom,
on our weekly video chat,
you echo those fibers again: *I hope*
you didn't get that from me. I'm so
sorry, Mom, but I think you know
what I got from you
is everything, and really, that's got
to be enough. I have patched it
for both of us
with alchemies you wouldn't trust.
I am still learning to enjoy
what we both are, this heritage
of humanity. We are here
just this once, and what I have
are these humble hands
which my daughter holds on Sunday mornings.
Gray eyes with short lashes.
Bunions and arthritic joints. What a glory
we both are.

Fulton Street Cemetery

Mulch-mounded barrow, hollow
of last summer's bones
where preachers carry clinical crowns
of paper, gravediggers' lips split,
counting hectares
and the fat mushrooms
at the feet of granite children.
We walk our linear communion
amid daffodil ballet, spring's shock
of chill cymbals. Coins
in our cold pockets are starships
for our innocence, the synchrony
of water and sky, our hands entangle,
becoming heretics amid this ash.
Beetles unravel skulls. Stars fever gold.
Here, where bodies remember wholeness,
a cat lathers puddles, watches high-flung finches.
We come to see the snow of pear blossoms
blown bone-bright, a glide of light
beside the footpath. What is done for bodies
is the science of hope,
grief stumbling into the yellow promise
of the bee, wakened early to her feast.

Plots

Look at a flourish chiseled in marble,
and count there each hour this woman spent
in childbirth, each time that man ran a hand
over the smooth cherrywood of his dining-room table.
Calculate that this child died at ten in the morning
and once, he prodded a large black ant with a stick
and watched it writhe there in the hard-packed dirt,
and that was the moment he understood regret.

Look into the branches of the biggest sweetgum,
at the crest of the cemetery, and see between its roots
the open earth and all the dead filling it—me and you
eternal as of yet but soon pared down to minerals,
spidering in every direction: stand beside the tombs.

Each slab shines with dull dates,
births and deaths which have nothing
to do with the act of living, the way the rain
hardened to ice on a Tuesday in March,
and this body, the one right below us,
had to step gingerly across the drive,
her weight cast forward, penguin-footed
as she came upon the garden
and the stiffened early lettuces which would thaw limp,
and how she put the hand of her body to each small green thing
that would never become, even as she planned
her reseeding for Saturday:
lettuce, and beets, too, and marigolds.

Catalpa Nonet

Corkscrew limbs, seedpod cigarillos,
a boon of freckled blooms, fissured
bark twirled in dance—at the park,
a fae door dwells in roots,
three steps leading to
heartwood's trick realm—
catalpa,
slump-backed
gnome.

From the Tower

The hills tip beneath me.
If I could stretch my arms
just a little wider, they'd be wings,
the long tail of rain upbending,
the thistles breaking free
and softening their tongues.
I have climbed wood traces
into places as blue as river
in summer, stretched like
a vital fiber, a darkness
that keeps ghosts from drifting.
The sun can't be denied
or defied, the great hurtling madness
that keeps carrots and beets
safe in their beds is not a thing
I can step away from, even on the edge,
the goblet sky ringing out
to be mined, asteroids
wishing for breath. Nothing allows
for such rebellion, for religion
or the woman on the corner begging
money for a baby she has only imagined
but who she believes in
all the more for that. The gray oak
is brittle and kind below my shoes,
and this precipice is a birth,
a human evolution, rising
on the ichthyosaur,
through ancient ocean, flyover zone.
I want to plunge,
plunge and live, green and bruise,
breathe and swallow. So many secrets
in the ladders of my bones—
hollow, tower-straight
all the way down, through limestone.
The only voice to answer my questions
is the one bubbling from my own larynx.
Here above the green, above waters,
hold the note long, valleys and comets
run through with ice.

Division, Spring

The meter attendant keys open parking meters
outside the church, bellies silver-full.
The peonies miracle. Ants crawl from bud-globes
and journey into the kitchen,
drawn by raw chicken on a Styrofoam tray. Feast
on birth, on death. The arrow of sun
splinters over sunflowers' black mouths.

The hophornbeams grow slow
in green strips along the hill,
ripening a row of nutlets
for the bobwhites and rabbits this fall.
The sky is scarred pink by plane trails,
the wooden bow of the horizon bends, wizened.

Hills are bodies: elbows, intestines, labia. Green
skin, skull roots. Dogs haul their owners toward home.
The elastic sweetness of hose water,
arcing over woodchip mulch.
A foot kicks brick from the garden bed,
and the ants below hurry to move their eggs
into some safer, deeper dark.

American Chestnut

They're stumps now.

Every decade or so, a shoot
rises
and is eaten up
by fungus.

America laments in its hungry way
as if nature schemed
all these fist-shaped
losses.

Sawtooth leaf and burred seedpod,
girdled and felled, taken
and lost. America
burns

the chestnut which stood
in its way
for America.
The doom of a tree is a hundred years long.

America
a flag
on a bare rock. A mountain
hollowed out.

A house whitewashed
and left open to wet flesh,
the fungus
of devouring.

Taking is easy,
all the way down to the ground.
The hillside is flayed. The deer have fled.
We are alone
in this debt of our own making,

America
singing lament,
singing
stranglehold.

The Garden on Wednesday

I. Insomnia

Nothing blooms this early but the squill,
which she hates for its pace,
the way it chokes out bluebells.
No other plants grow from that patch

all summer long.
Dead ground. The half-dead trees
loiter like night-shifters at dawn
along the wire fence. Barely

on their feet. A pile
of leaves from last fall
chokes sunlight. The soil
shifts, compacted by a sprawl

of Alabama jumper worms infesting
the yard. The dogwood is all twigs.

II. Resurrection

The garlic she planted in cold beds
finally shoots green as the daylilies
overtake the junk mound by the shed,
grassy blades potent as licorice.

She drags a fallen maple limb
from the pond and sees the first spiral
of a hosta. Iris knives shake off ice skims.
The moss roars slow toward light.

Here marks echinacea and sweet pea,
conjuring color from composted scraps.
Here, the phlox schemes butterfly and bee.
All below the dirt, seeming dead, except

for an imperceptible inching higher
towards spring rain's quiet fire.

Tides Glosa

The Moon is distant from the Sea –
And yet, with Amber Hands –
She leads Him – docile as a Boy –
Along appointed Sands –

— Emily Dickinson

Heat creeps up ductwork
in the old house
and the bracts of the Douglas fir
hold fast to their cones, three-taloned claws.
While the girl is at school,
her mother checks in books
at the library, sorts titles on carts,
answers phone calls and sends faxes.
One's breath to the other is spider-silk, distant as
the moon is distant from the sea.

All day, cars drive by the empty apartment.
The water in the mother's glass on the nightstand
pulses faintly to the neighbor's music.
The girl's pillow has slipped onto the carpet.
Her pajamas lie in a pile
just outside the bathroom door.
They've left the cutting board out
from an apple snack last night.
The day is a cold wall,
and yet, with amber hands,

the sun pulls clouds
like a load of whites from the dryer.
In this city, how many
have died today? And how many
in other cities, metal
rooted through chests?
In yew bushes outside the school,
a robin outwaits the rain.
The girl draws a fish on construction paper, and
she leads him, docile as a boy,

into the shallows of a salty lake.
Her mother is gone
to some other continent
where she sews thought
into book bindings. The fish
on paper swims close lines,

water shallow, and too blue.
The thread tightens, mother
and child reaching into opposite tides
along appointed sands.

How To Be Saved, If You Are a Body

A fallow field filled with deadnettle,
the slope to the ditch tumbling in violets,
unmown yards rising up in henbit.
And the jagged sidewalk where I plod
over mud puddles. And the black chest
in the laundry room where I sit
while my husband shrugs on his wool jacket,
and with it, the weight of all days.

How long since I walked along a river?
Since the herons threatened with their sword-beaks,
their legs tensed for the immense effort
of flight? Am I lost or saved beside the waters?
The starlings grubbing
between bright blots of spring beauties.

I want to enter all things as a child
lying on her stomach with her head in the open arch
of oak roots. To open the red of every tulip
like a tongue between teeth, to find the space
where the universe is, all its immensity
bound and springing up from one sticky stamen.
I am redeemed inside the daffodil's cup
and the star of the periwinkle.

My body is lost among pine boards
and found in the damp cool of the garage
as I grip trowel and pink plastic pot,
as I sow cosmos and zinnias with my daughter
out on the crumbling cement steps.
The cardinal sings loud as liturgy,
a recitation of creed, a salvation story.

Because

The crocus have opened wide
and stuck out their orange tongues.
Up in the sky,
8,000 planes fling bodies over oceans
and today, not one of them crashes.
The starlings stuff straw into their beaks;
they've got plans, and so do
the thousands of students in this city
studying for final exams,
fingering vibrating cell phones in their pockets.
At the greenhouse, employees haul seedlings
under grow lights
and spritz tropical plants. The air smells of fertilizer
and peat, oxygen-soaked.
The river delivers pesticides and carp,
but also the fertile bodies of salmon.
Generations open wet eyes
while ants plan new schematics.
A painter blocks out her canvas,
a child writes her first word—her name—
and with that, everything begins, new again,
our lungs fill again, the page waiting
for what the hand will make of it.

Incorruptible

Mahogany tree, you hold
dry above the lines
of broken blue sea.

Rows of tropical arbor,
sunscreen
and baseball-cap ardor,

US-claimed islands
of amputated voting rights,
staked rows of seedlings,

plantation sugar
and charcoal, cigarbox cedar
and mahogany.

Over-harvested shine,
each waxen petal
returns red in southern spring.

The tide,
the spines of ships,
Swietenia mahagoni

as fortepiano and the wooden bars
of marimba, as peeled layers
of a Gibson Les Paul,

as the splintered hull
which harbored
a young John F. Kennedy.

Did I once, in the Gulf,
hold my child hand
to your sharp dark?

Endangered and sheltering,
picked piecemeal from ships' cabins
and railroad parlor cars.

You harbor
what returns after
and what came before.

The Diver

I pick dried stalks
of Queen Anne's lace from flower beds,
sort leaf litter with delicate hands.
Springtails sing their bodies through mulch
as caterpillars wake along bark rifts. Flowers
skeletons of themselves,
fleshy bulbs which know season
the way a cat knows sunlight.
Squirrels dig in the compost
lit up with secrets, like the treasure box
in second grade, my arm reaching in to the elbow.
I know what belongs.
I parse, I winnow.

I stretch my neck, thinking of the diver at the high-school pool,
how even his toes were wound tight
as he poised for a great leap, the loud flap
of the board, and all the air,
that solitude of turning body, time
stretched open like an iris,
the quick eternity
before the bloom of water, foam and laughter.

Treasure

Behind a rundown ranch on Ward Street, two pet rabbits
are allowed to roam free. We walk by; they
are always there. Across the street,
a woman in a gray hoodie
hauls a big bag of clothes to the curb,
and a cheap folding papasan.
It's spring clean-up week in town,
and no one seems lonely.
A man in farmers' overalls
puts three red stools and a cushionless couch
of 90's-era vintage at the end of his driveway.
The spendthrift and stone-broke trade castoffs
like ragged pennies, a Wheel of Fortune spinning
prizes—scrap metal, cotton dresses, musty children's books.
Lilacs bob their heavy heads at the loud pickups
pulling flatbed trailers stacked high
with broken washers and kids' Walmart bikes. Odin's raven
caws from a high branch in the empress tree,
leafless, but filling with coronas of purple and gold.
From inside this cloud-and-concrete pearl, I feel myself falling
into folds of memory, falling across the town square
with the never-wound clock, falling as water
into brimful fields, interim lakes.
My friend writes, *What an awful time to* have *to find a job.*
For the first time this week, we find the rabbits fenced
along with three rabbit kittens—white, sorcerous,
their suspicious ruby eyes
daring us toward butterweed ditches.

Fable in which you are a barn animal and I am a carnivore

Suppose, you say, *it began with the chickens,*
the way one wing raised
could unbalance,
the way they learned
to tilt their heads
in a concession to gravity, all at once.

Yes! I like it, I say.
The pleasure of synchronicity.

The pigs, being dominant
in cognition, would be next.
They might listen to the rain
and learn rhythm
from the downspout.

Music, it seemed to you,
would be a matter of curled tail
and the scent of hay.
The cows would sing, without
meaning to.

I am entranced now: *And the dark star*
on the forehead of a pregnant heifer
would pulse, and she would moan
the river into the valley.

You think this lovely, but obtuse.
You say, *All night long, the fireflies*
make love to the mist,

and in the morning,
I interrupt,
the fox carries the music away,
warm between her jaws.

Grandma Dory's Pond

The edge scallops into the muddy beach like a fish scale.
My daughter toes in, her foam sandals smooshing between lake weeds
and black mussels. It's hot, the water's tepid. The landscape
is three flat planes: gravel, corn, and soybeans. The house
and a row of arborvitae block fields to the west. Between stalks,
killdeer sound out afternoon light, a thunderhead's spill of darkness
to the south. My daughter moves through the water, buoyant and awkward,
clambers onto the deck, jumps back in the pond. Bluegills and algae whirl off stones.
My mother-in-law wanders down the hill to the shed
where a pair of mud-crusted boots grow stiff with age. She finds an inflatable raft,
one my husband remembers from childhood summers here.
He is lifeguard today in his swim trunks, dry for now but keeping an eye
on the tan, blonde girl who screeches as her sandal wriggles free
and floats on the surface like a rainbow duckling.
Cottonwoods' green coins shimmer in a whipped wind.
The old lapdog comes down to the bank to drink.
I sit beside the oldest mother here, who talks of her husband,
eight-years-gone now. Some of his woodworking tools are still in the shed,
but his shotgun was passed off to his daughter. She used it this spring
to shoot a raccoon who'd been after the strawberries.
Thunder is closer now. We go in, and the girl showers
in the lost husband's bathroom. I open the door to the spare bedroom—the quilting room—
where I nursed my daughter after the funeral. At Christmas
two years ago I sliced open my finger with a pocketknife
and had to lay down in the white chapel of this hallway, beside the washer and dryer,
so I wouldn't pass out. My daughter comes from the shower now, warm and wet,
still smelling just a little of the pond's green. I wrap her in a towel
the same silver as the thunderhead, a soft remembering, frayed with giving.
My husband naps in his grandfather's easy chair,
but I am still uneasy here, even after all this time. I look out
at the rain-starred pond, the velveteen storm.
The crops sway, synchronous dancers. Ohio breathes in a wet cough,
opens over me, and spills in deep.

Call It Peace

when was it
        all the Apple River's cows
                would low evening
                over the hillcrest and into my bed

crack open the north window

        all the day creeps in
        the sound of corn growing

grain trucks and a semi full of sows
                who will speak for the Midwest

        flyover plains
        my driftless corner
I would dream into farms

                come to the milking
                hides of mist and hoarfrost
        the bank-mud hooved deep

                make a childhood
        from nitrogen-green fields
the lullaby of pasture oaks

Oak Abecedarian

Arched over the county road, oaks blind the curve, a roil of
branches where raccoons cross, mother followed by small ones, on a night
crowned with humid hope. We brake, sudden, and see the glowing eye, not
dead, but could have been, may yet be. What
evolves to stand still? To bury? To
forest in spirals of dense shade, harboring milkcap mushrooms and wasp larvae like
gospel? I wind my hands into oaks' roughness, ask what they
hide between nut caps and galls. I hear their deliberation,
insects weaving through oakmoss, claws of limbs like those where
Joab found Absalom tangled. Oak strength, placid abettor of slaughters. A
keystone tree, oak opens to the hide-and-seek of green, grows expansive. The
long stretch of oak's body shivers thousands of acorns during
mast seasons, sidewalks stained sienna through slow seeping, oak the
north star of persistence. What the oak knits over centuries, we ax in hours,
one in ten thousand acorns reseeding what we have taken. Learn
patience from this. Glory is an oak which we let be.
Quercus, queen tree, heart of parks and prairie-forest borders. Children
read in oak leaves a hundred stories. Mystic fortress of belief, oak is
solid in a way which defies decay. Time is
textured by oak: gray, green. Branches of snow, of butterfly. We
uproot oak for furniture, to sweeten wine, to swing, to pound drum. We
venerate and eviscerate. Under oak men buried gods and
women buried still infants. Bones between roots,
xylem sipped slow by cicada nymphs. Oak trunks make covenant a hundred
years at a time, the sacred center, the
zapis where we preach the secret of our dreams.

Fairy Stories

A ceramic pig, a paper box,
a fold of soft blue and the open white
of new diapers. I was invoked fat
and pink and quiet, good
in my mystic crib,
in my thin plastic car seat,
the drive to Ohio, my mother's descent
from happiness in that damask-dark apartment
with three small children.
I drank milk ten months, ceremony
of sweet, my brothers
pausing to touch my hand,
baby of discomfort, father
in lecture halls,
wishing for the damp basement
where he learned the form
of earth in his hands. My spell
was the long corridor of highway,
the hill-buried town,
the coral root of cancer in my toddler neck.
Curse of summer, curse of purple curtains,
the plaster ceiling peeled away
in dry scabs, this upper room
of my enchantment.
I charmed my body into valleys,
bewitched tumbles of clover
and lamb's ear. The lake drew deep,
crevice of river, the hills
pulled by moon
in tide. I was needle-born
and scalpel honed,
a trance of sanitized sheets,
a wonder of number
which washed my mother
barren. The gift which bore me
was the weight of peonies in June,
the folds of my infant wrists,
and a long white gown
from which water woke me.
The mercy of palm, of gasoline,
of plastic dolls. I curled
tight, fiddlehead-tender,
holding a glow-in-the-dark pony.
What fortune to survive,
thinking still of the end
which was, which will be,
the messy work of sparrows and grubs.

Atlas of Being

You make a map of the world,
close your eyes,
and put your finger anywhere,
that's it, you say
to this home of globe.
A map is like a book, but
where a book demands and dominates,
a map asks to be scried, mastered.
The oceans circle your finger,
lap you with sundog tongues.
The allium rise like planets
to orbit the green rectangle of yard.
Wonder seeps in you, stark as ink.
You put on your shoes and walk into the map.
The street is blue and easy;
the robins tuft their crowns into flattops.
What the map needs, you think, are trees.
The way paper is more receptive to color
if it's got a bit of tooth. Texture is a matter for the eye
as much as the hand. How, through the bus window,
the accordion folds of new elm leaves
sawtooth shades of green into a grin.
You put your hand to your neck,
you are a red pin, stuck deep,
you put your finger to your lip,
the sound of destination spiraling out,
midnight lightness,
a place to call your body
into the shape of being.

Willow

The underbelly of the lake
shines green on fish and stones.
Chlorophyll glows
as blue filters in, the gold of summer softening.

The willow holds the earth
from giving way to water,
wind tearing at the leafy hair, a tendril
pulled away, rooting now on the far shore.

Below the mirror which sky makes of water,
something beyond your own skin
grows and names you Mother,
the way clouds give birth to the weeds.

The way seeds are just a part of you
which you have to let go.

Godliness

In microarthropods and caterpillars
munching leaf decay,
in nematodes and protozoa,
clay layered like filo, God is.
A thin biopsy of star,
a green wink of precious stone.
Root-cellar jars lined in scum,
cool and clean beneath sealed lids.
The deep tap, spirit
in tectonic plates,
delivering cities into rivers.
Below boulders, water
runs clear, filtered by limestone beds,
the dark surge, aquifer-holy.
Why not a religion of eel and beetle,
stone cracked, mud seeping?
Spit in the gravel
and God's finger reaches in.
Cavern revelation, coal prayer,
the miracle of metamorphism.
God, six-legged, trapped
in amber. Gold as that,
archaeological and unrefined,
God of the brown marrow
from which we bloom.

Detritus

Worlds are altered rather than destroyed.

— Democritus

The tree of heaven spills like fountain
from a caved-in roof,
thistles shocking the limestone foundation
with their purple brushes.
I have come to see this ruin.
To pick my way along graveled path
and pitched concrete
to the place where the world
wins itself back. Raccoons and feral cats
scar each others' flesh nightlong,
and grasses lining the chain-link fence seed
and reseed, metal sharp as a coyote's spine
amid inflorescences.
That which destroys what we've built
is also what saves us, not as ourselves
but as vine, rainwater, spider-sac—life
in the thousands, bursting through
the thin membranes of our walls.

How satisfied are you with each of the following in your city?

Water: ★★★

Osmosis filtered, it shines diamond. But the creek water at Wilcox Park is mucking up the invertebrates. And the leeches love our ankles. Still, I am a water balloon, a praise of lakes, waves slapping my parents' aluminum canoe while I sleep below the yoke and they dip us across Lake Le-Aqua-Na. Asian carp are a cheek full of slender bone. The far-off salty arms of the Atlantic pull more and more of me into salt each year.

Traffic: ★

No matter how carefully I check my blind spot, I can't keep cars from drifting into my bumper. Box trucks and buses shear mirrors from parked SUVs, leaving love notes tucked beneath windshield wipers. The jam to cross the bridge is ant-steady, and houses beside the highway fall asleep to the white noise of mufflers and engine braking. As I descend the hill into town, the terrain recedes to brick. All the things we've pulled from the earth to burn have become hard, red, unbreathable.

Greenspace: ★★★★

Even the Callery pears are hopeful, lining mulched strips of mud between asphalt and concrete, though in spring they stink of rotting fish. Anything reaching toward the unlikely blue: peony, barberry, begonia, mum. Ginkgoes and Norway maple cultivars. The grass grows slick with magnolia petals. I pull my cap lower, shielding my face from sun at trees' crowns. The silver of something which reaches below this scabbed land. I see only the mouth of leaves. The buried body is what saves me.

Cottonwood Music

after "ode to flute" by Ross Gay

The teeth of the tree know
the way clouds are seeds,

the way seeds
are rain in reverse. Cottonwood

kneels in river silt,
sings rings of a thousand beaver mouths.

Twigs twirl leafy hips in wind. Waft of white
June, skin-soft drift.

Cottonwood stretches, ditch-deep,
lamb's ear, the silver pyre and purple bloom.

I enter the bark and return as root.
The edge of the wheat sea

is this one tree
this fence line and pebble bed,

jagged green shovels
welcoming lung and flute.

September River

Beneath stone, the spine of water
runs between banks
of cottonwood and birch,
a current, splitting death in two:
the first yellow leaves of autumn eddy-swirled;
the late-season blackfly larvae
springing in shallows.

Braids of moss cling to the scapula
of hill. The grass is rebuilt in gold,
summer's end shining. Autumn
is more a twig buried in soil
than a gravestone. Not as final
as it appears from six feet away.

The river stitches world to world
with the cord of these little deaths.
Honeysuckle roots shifting sand
around wet tendrils. Mice
learning the edges of harvest,
small fur in the water. Beetle
iridescent blue on silt-colored water,
remembering the sky. Rain
turning them all to shining stone.

The Sweetness of Honey Locusts

I ride my bike over leaflets, a rain,
a fluttering wake, a living yellow, ride
and breathe hard, like *postpandemic*
is a word I can own, like *after*
is a concept as well defined as *café*
or *husband* or *inertia*. Thorn and
pulp, the rasp of zigzag branches,
mask fluttering from my pocket.

Cars spew vivid petals, three dead deer
putrefy as I climb the hill, descend fern-like
on my bike, a zoom of isolation,
rooms peopled by nobody, or everyone
except me. Two years we have breathed alone,
locust branches grown from our lungs,
returned now as seed pods,
sweetish, leathery, tannin-rich.

One crooked body overlaps another,
gathering gray against the yellow fall,
gathering days like dropped limbs,
subsumed by bramble, skittered in ditches.
The color of loss is bright against the sky,
sap at the hewing,
what is left growing wild as weeds,
out-competing death. Wanted creatures need no thorns.

The soil is thin and wet and *post*
means to bury deep, to stand, rot-resistant,
the nature of a spoken body.
Limb plucks skin, and we become whole
along the line where we were touched.
In a field where purple grasses once grew
a thicket of fierce thorns
germinates future in honey-thick wombs.

Constellation

The hardpacked dirt of the alley
is polished by the soles
of our feet. Dark stone lines the drive,
fish-scale smooth. In black silhouette,
the wooden ribs of a half-built home
knit together out of the hillside.
If we cracked the bedrock below,
would we find promise, ore?
Just beyond our own yard,
the gravel edge meets uneven earth, a fence
of metal mesh, a layer of brick.
What we call inside is here,
between our cupped hands. And out
are the stars, the water mains,
the constellations of traffic
and night-lit office buildings.
We travel the edge,
let the yew trees hold our secrets
deep in their poison boughs.

Memorial

Think of your childhood bed,
the empty Blue Bunny tub on the floor
beside you, how you heaved into it,
the way it captured and muffled
your breathing. Remember
the small ceramic cup with blue flowers
that your mother or father filled
with lemon-lime soda. Remember how thirsty you were,
how you thought the fizzy sweetness could quench
all the wrongness inside of you. And the cold washcloth
pressed to your forehead, the damp sheets,
your lamp with the pink and green quilted shade.
Outside, semi trucks hurried through town,
rattled the loose plaster of your second-story ceiling.
You could see the neighbors' TV
through the eave window. Remember
how the cup was never empty, not when you needed it.
And how someone carried the plastic tub
down the stairs and dumped it in the toilet
while you slept. Your brother
wheeled the little white TV into your room.
You watched rented VHS tapes
which he picked out for you after school. Remember how bright
the cup's blue flowers were when you woke in the night,
and the house was cold and quiet. You wore your PJs
for three days straight, did not brush your hair
or your teeth. Stomach acid etched small inlets
that would later become cavities and crowns.
In the morning, you held the mercury thermometer
below your tongue. The cup was gone then—
and you thought for a moment
that your parents must be magic, the way things appeared
one moment, and then were gone. The cloth, the cup,
the extra blanket which you pulled up to your neck
and then tossed onto the floor. Grape-flavored Tylenol.
And then the cup was back, small bubbles clinging
to its glazed walls. Remember how the bed
weighed anchor and drifted past all the people
you loved most. You were not a passenger
but the sail, catching in your leaflike body
the memory of wind, baling the rest of you
over the edge of your universe. A gentle wave
of used tissues, the TV remote, schoolbooks,
your pink rabbit with felt flowers sewed
between her front paws. A hand hoisted you
up the post of your headboard. The cup

was stitched into a corner of your body. It was filled, again and again, with cool cure, with the moon turned liquid, and from it you filled and emptied and filled your stomach.

Division, Fall

Only the library desk separates us
as he mops his forehead
with the chambray shirt draped across his shoulders.
I fold my hands, a humid cage between my palms.
Across town, a woman steers her mobility chair
over Division Avenue, a van turns left.
She dies before the driver even unbuckles their seatbelt.

And in the river, fish with gill disease
drift in the rapids. A heron
reflects gray onto gray water. The pond frogs
suffocate in algae bloom.
Nothing between us but aerosols
and CO2. The drape of traffic,

newsfeeds of bullet and hurricane.
The bus empties. We're not sorry, not at all,
the way my smile mutes my tongue,
the way the blanket drapes
across her chest, the way he speaks
without having seen
my hands at all.

Norway Maple Stand

Like pencils crowded in a jar
and fanning toward kitchen cupboards,
erasers anchoring in glass, bodies rising
into fine points which seem to gleam
when light casts through the cloudy pane
of the south-facing window: various,
some taller, some with superior graphite
for a note or a doodle while on hold with the electric company,
our favorite autumn yellow, school-yellow No. 2s,
dumped from backpacks onto the dining room table
and relocated here to huddle into a forest
of all the things we dared etch—
a pair of scissors slung lightly between,
the grace of chosen pruning,
paper-scrap corymbs of chartreuse blooms,
silent, waiting for need, the water
of notated recipes, amended schedules,
the air around their striving barrels asks for hands,
their thin shadows branch
into a picnic of light below the windowsill.

Inheritance

My grandmother's fingers are knobbed and crooked, her small feet
like tree roots, her body a finality—
bladder, breasts, collar, hip, labor-worn breath.
I wish she knew something I don't
as she kneels in the soft pebbles of her greenhouse,
a prayer to muscle, as she places hand to potting soil,
breathes in the chalky humidity. She fingers
the asparagus fern, which was her mother's.
How close she is to what lives,
to color churned bright from water and decay.
I want her to tell me that we are golden as oak blossoms in spring.
I want to shiver her last words into blessing,
infant ghost, baby saint. Just say there's something
to learn from death. She turns to my nine-year-old daughter
and says my name. She cannot rise from her place by the fern,
her root. Unfair of me to wish for answers. Her mind
grows as opaque as the ivory tusks
she brought home from Ethiopia in her first year of marriage.
My brother and father and husband
guide her to the easy chair, and she watches
as they roll her piano down the driveway and load it in the truck.
It arrives in my living room on my daughter's birthday,
and her ten-year-old fingers are aerial shadows
of my grandmother's hands
as she skims the black and white bones, as my grandmother
breathes in, and waits, with little patience.
What dream lingers, in the end? Perhaps
life is not brief. But it is not long either. Perpetual
and perishing, like daylight
or mosquitoes. A cutting from the fern,
building new roots from ancient memory.

Feast

The carving knife
wobbled at the edge of the counter,
the silver blade seeming almost liquid
as it bent the light of the kitchen.
But as it fell, the weight of it
pulled sharpness solid,
embedding in my grandfather's socked toe.
My mother bundled him into a wooden chair,
my father slid an aluminum bowl
meant for drippings below the injured foot.
Gentle blood plashing into the bowl.
The white sock discarded, rosebud
and cotton. His eyes closed around the pain,
the room burnt-sugar sweet
from baking yams. Three generations
bent over the filling bowl,
creating an arched dome
of sanctuary, the blood
looking much like the maple leaves outside,
brilliant, opaque, aflame.
Seeming more alive now in perishing
than they had all summer long.

Taking Out the Trash on Tuesday Night

I stand in the gravel, wrapping my arms tight
around me. The sky is not so empty as it seems.
Just today, it was filled with rain
as the squirrels carried mouthfuls of leaves
up the neighbors' oak for nest-building.

The silence is a milk-splash of fog
and star, the moon already set.
Nights like this one are heavy, almost as if
our planet has drifted from the sun and rolled
under the bed between dust bunnies
and the box of sweaters.

I think of the books crowded on the living room shelf,
of paper nests, nests of words. Of the nest
of my mind, how I fluff the doubt snug
in the corners so that I can sleep at night.

The owls choose to wake and sleep
in proper intervals, unconcerned with doubt.
Need is incessant that way. What is there to do
but hunt, consume, and breed?

The night is foreign to me now,
a void quiet. Inside the house, I am missed.
Someone comes to check on me and calls my name
from the back door. I walk in, warm again,

separate again. The rain starts in again
as I wipe my feet on the rug. I pick up a dish towel
and contemplate the dinnerware, warm
and clean and empty.

Earth to Earth

I usually hold her hand
at the crosswalk
but today it's raining
I'm holding my umbrella
she's holding hers
and we reach the light
halfway through the walk signal
the left turners in full swing
she steps
into the white road
I reach for anything at all
grab the seams on her backpack
and jerk
as a bus turns in front of us
I hold her wrist
umbrella-tangle
so tight so long after we cross
she asks me to let go
my fear
clenching her hard enough to hurt
how can I keep her safe

this is October
the time to remember our dead
cracking knee joints
dirt dug deep
scars in gravel roads
we are not safe
and we hold too tight
sky flooding us
the grass drowning
basement of centipedes and spiders
the bodies of what was
the folder of papers
which were once important

I hold her knit mitten in my black glove
marigold bright
the blue of school-day mornings
peanut butter crackers
and the rain
the cemetery wall tall and still
all the way down Fountain Street
her rubber boots fevering the puddles

what I would give
to run like that
inches deep in mud
and then track it all through the house
like a living thing
cold and sure as splashing

The apple

sunsets in the black bowl
between mangos
and Anjou pears.
A mile, a thousand
miles from the tree. Sweet white blossoms.
A hand inverting the fruit,
turning it from branch.
The apple in my bowl
bruises against ceramic.
The memory of its orchard
tastes blue as sky. Cloud-filled, bumblebee.
Green rows glorying all hot long, all grasshopper
and windstorm. As much as the tree
made the apple, so did we.
The taste of our mouths. Pink tongues.
The bite of a grafted body,
the healthy rootstock, limbs of Honeycrisp
clones. From the bowl, the apple can see me
with my morning toast,
can see me load and unload the dishwasher,
the glint of the window, the fresh yard
where yucca stalks thicken
and sunflowers dream of seeds.
The earth below the house pulses with roots,
with unripe fruit.
The apple waits, long into the night.

The Split Season

The sycamores
are an archery of limbs.
With the first feeble snow,
the privacy of green
slips from the hawthorn.
Pokeweed and wild phlox
wither. This is the stripped season,
the naked gray catalog of sleep.
Rain bends into ice, the yard
a silver palace. The mice
and caterpillars dream of our slow feet
on snow. I have put away
my bicycle, I have pulled on
thick socks. Light spills in yellow blocks
across the empty chest of the street.

What has been salvaged
from the rocky summer garden?
A man in a gray coat stumbles the cold Wednesday
through my yard, over to my recycling bin,
searching for refundables.
Along the house foundation, dirt
instructs the leaves in the art of decay.

The highway fills with carbon dioxide
and desire. The charitable shelters fill with need,
a hundred cold hands. On my own cold counter,
green bananas ripen, and apples
wither like icy hillsides.
I November into the freeze.
The buried tulip bulbs. Waters rise,
but not here. And elsewhere, fires.
I turn the heat up, hear the gas catch
in the furnace. I boil water for tea,
and dream the snow clean, the city quiet.

Diminishing Returns

The oceans are the last holdout for cold weather,
the sky divided, the dune grasses ragged,

the rags of sand multiplying into sky.
I clutch the end of the world like a kite string,

the end a clutch of days strung in flood,
the horizon glinting glass-bottle clouds,

the horizon bent over trash islands, plastic-bottle bound,
and because of this, you put your ear to my collarbone,

because of this, you ask the well of my collarbone
to be your heartbeat's sea. I want to

beat the heart of the sea red. I want to
conjure permafrost below our atmospheric dome,

hold you permafrost long, conjure gray bones of ice,
our oceans cold with the last glacial dregs.

False Cedar

Gray light, twilight, darkening and cold.
Redcedars seed, invade farm pastures,
spread limbs over prairie grasses.

But come in close, crush a redcedar berry the color of sky,
inhale the astringent fragrance. Walk beneath redcedar trees,
alley gravel crunching, brush hands through scaled leaves. Sigh,
and it will return the breath, fragranced and robust.

Redcedar, tolerant of sand, rock, clay, drought, and cold:
in fire, flames ladder through its lower branches
to consume the offering in one glorious gulp.

Farmers singe its branches to protect pastures,
each green sheath peeled back and back
until the whole of the tree is orange as flame,
scorched dry, skinned in charcoal.

The waxwings rise on the hot vapors
with redcedar seeds in their bellies,
carrying the tree like a secret egg into another life.

Snow

how blue a road seems
in winter sunlight

the way the days end
before we understand them

and how the last blue before dark
is warmer than blue should be

blue is what the sky makes of angels
snow-bound and broken

fragile as the new moon
eleven white dunes and all our footprints

icy brick walks and plowed mounds on the berm
our clothes pressed flat as Sunday white

try to find a blue bluer than white
each drift a lick of sugar on glass

the snow unfetters the clouds
how blue a road seems

without the green encroaching
without dandelions and mock strawberries

and the warmth
where blue can't dance

where white melts into gray
and feeds this brightness

When I Die

Lay me on the red-needle understory
of an eastern hemlock grove.

Rest my head below a canopy of maples,
amid trillium and Dutchman's breeches.

Let me look last at the shagbark hickory,
straight and ragged. Roots, roots,

this is a place I would have me become.
The spruce dips its branches into me.

The oak covers me in acorn caps.
The forest is not benevolent,

but the way it lives feels to me
like salvation.

Brush me against fungi.
Litter me with pollen.

I am not afraid of all this green,
of millipedes and roly-poly bugs.

Sweet as cherry, strong as ironwood,
silver as beech. The trees sing water

to the leaves. Lay me here at the end,
beside persistent, blighted chestnut.

To be pelted with the walnut's hostility.
I am unafraid to become.

And in the fall, the yellow honey locust,
the sassafras, the slippery elm,

and fir resin, sealing shut the future,
readying for flame.

About The Author

Hannah Marshall lives in Grand Rapids, Michigan, where she works at the public library. Marshall's poems have been published in The Best American Poetry, New Ohio Review, The American Journal of Poetry, Four Way Review, Poetry Daily, and elsewhere. She received her MFA in creative writing from Converse University.

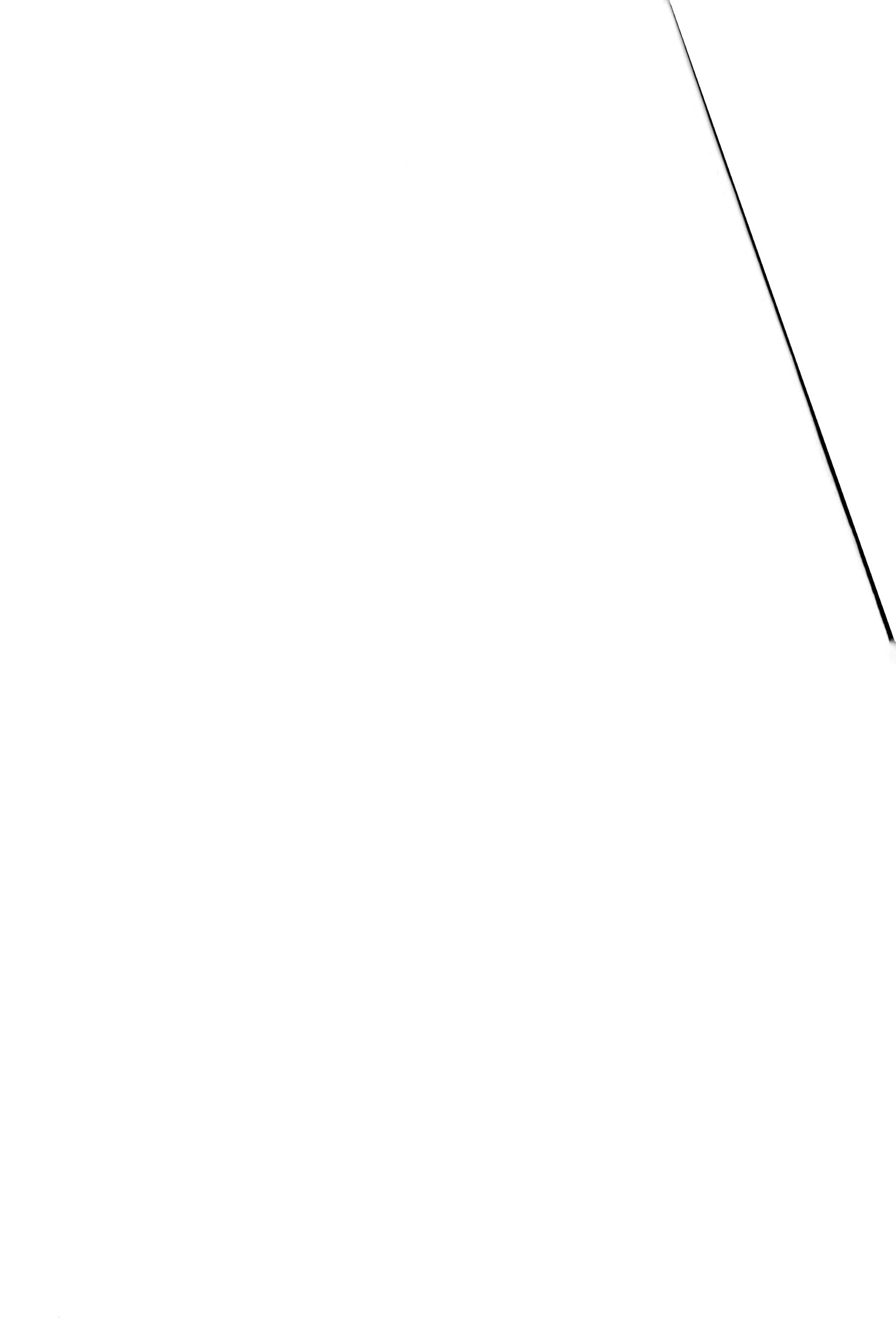

www.ingramcontent.com/pod-product-compliance
Lightning Source LLC
LaVergne TN
LVHW060628110826
845147LV00015B/961

9781638042280